Someone who really does know how you feel

(A book about my experience with depression, self-harm and anxiety in the Priory)

James Allen

DEDICATION

"To everyone who thinks they are alone, and can't find a way out"

CONTENTS

1. THE FIRST NIGHT IS ALWAYS THE HARDEST.

So, he was being admitted. As he climbed back into his mum's car he could feel the panic and anxiety taking a hold of him. It was as if someone had waited for the green light to click ready on an iron and now held it hard agents his chest.

The car pulled away from the curb, radio off so as not to trigger any emotions. The engine could be heard over the sat nav barking instructions loud and clear "in one hundred meters take the next left". The night was dark, lights flashing fast and bright outside the passenger window. Thoughts going off like a firework display in his head, bang after bang, all self-control had now been lost. Images of the Priory bustled their way to the forefront of his mind. Straight jackets and screaming...Was he really that bad? "yes" came a voice from the darkness in his mind. It had been the one question that had convinced him, even in his current state. "Are you safe to be left alone" the doctor had asked pen in hand. The answer was no. The self-harm had gone too far out of control now, he had begun to fear each cut was just counting down to his last. The one that would clear his head of these demons and memory's forever. His end game. Although he knew he had so much to live for he didn't care anymore. It didn't matter if the

1

positives and consequences tipped the right way, he wanted to be selfish for the first time. He wanted out.

Glancing down at the small navigation display his heart rate instantly tripled, he could actually feel it against his chest. Zero point one miles to destination. Before he knew it, he could read the large green sign "Woodbourne Hospital". As he forced himself out of the car and into the cold February wind that began hitting hard against him, he was numb. Walking in head down he could hear a voice in the distance, his mum asking the receptionist where we needed to go. Once directed to a waiting area he took note of his surroundings, it was clean and warm he thought. After what felt like seconds he was meet by a male nurse wearing a large smile.

All walking together they glided along to the wards entrance. As he approached the glass he could see people gathered in the lobby area, panic, nerves and anxiety now at breaking point. The nurses fob beeped loudly and the magnetic door released, "this is it" he said to himself. He was introduced to a member of staff and two inpatients stood chatting and laughing on the stairs. Hand shaking uncontrollably, he reached out and introduced himself, his voice a mere whisper. Immediately his head dropped back to the floor, heart beating as if he had just crossed a finish line. His eyes however managed to glance around and pick up small details, the welcome sign printed onto a fresh looking wooden plaque, the new clean carpet, modern and comfortable furniture. Most importantly the informality. Unless he was now completely delusional the two patients he had just meet were not wearing straight jackets, the atmosphere warm and friendly, not a scream to be heard. As he sat in what may be his room for the next few weeks he was vividly reminded of a four-star hotel, the decor, bed, fresh smell of linen there was even an on-suite bathroom to match. This was so far from his expectations, he could at least be comfortable here. A knock on the door asked if he wanted anything to eat. Before he could open his mouth, his mother did what all mothers tend to do, "yes please, he hasn't eaten anything all day" she replied, the woman acknowledged with a smile and clicked the door shut. "No canteen?" he said allowed. So far, this place seemed much more like a home than a hospital. Next to introduce themselves was the night staff nurse, a more pleasant and calming introduction could not have been possible. Questions were asked, boxes were ticked and his name signed more than a premier league footballer after a big match. A full medical checkup followed. He was guided upstairs to the clinic and all the normal observations were made. This was always going to be difficult and somewhat uncomfortable having to take your top off for the ECG, but he was talked through every action and even the small talk actually reassured him.

The hardest part followed, saying goodbye to his mum. He knew only he could solve this situation and work hard to fix and contain these demons inside his head but she offered a comfort blanket, a shield from reality. Tears began to flow down his cheek one by one, "I'll see you tomorrow" she whispered in his ear as they embraced, "you will be fine, I know it" she said with a confidence he could see was a front just for him. The door shut with a clunk. He felt as though he was standing alone in an empty storage unit, every light burnt out. Pitch black. Darkness surrounding him like a heavy fog. He walked backed to his room quickly trying to hold back more tears. All he wanted to do was cut, cut himself over and over again self-harming his way to a false sanctuary, however standing now in the centre of his room he knew this was not possible. A knock again "we have a goodnight group at half past nine, everyone sits and talks about their day, you don't have to attend if you don't want to" He didn't want to, instead he wanted to be laying in bed, letting the thoughts that had brought him here eat away at his mind and sanity.

When half past nine finally struck it was with another knock and yet another smile, This time a young woman in her twenty's. She introduced herself and pronounced that goodnight group was about to begin. With every will in his body screaming at him to stay isolated "stay in bed, close your eyes" his demons bellowed in his head. To this day he does not know where he mustered the courage and energy to get himself out of that bed and follow the woman into a room full of people he didn't know. It was in fact the best decision he ever made. He was not alone. He was not ALONE.

Slowly as each patient, person soon to be friend spoke about their day, opening up to everyone, lights began to flick on in the storage unit. He could see people appearing one by one, the male nurse that had greeted him, the night nurse, the young lady, person after person now stood next to him. Stronger together. Once over he returned to his room undressed and got into bed, his head containing a small, incredibly tiny little bit of light and hope that before now had not been there at all. Before now it had not even been a possibility or conceivable to him. Little did he know that in the days to follow that light slowly gets brighter and brighter. Don't be discouraged or give up hope, you are not alone. That light may well flicker on and off but it is there, embrace it with both hands, wind up the power if you have to, just stay in the light. It gives you a new-found ability and enables you to see all these people you didn't know were stood next to you shoulder to shoulder the entire time. People that really do have the capability to save your life.

Just know that the first night is always the hardest.

2. THE MAN WITH ALL THE JOKES.

As he sat there hot and sweeting, the small living room filled with people bent over in laughter. His mind whizzing round like a high speed roller-coaster, desperately looking, searching for the next joke to preform..." 1 must keep them laughing" he said to himself. After another ten or so minuets of everyone bent over in hysterics at his funniness, whit and somewhat cheeky comments the room began to clear. One by one they all bid him goodnight, he made a few more passing jokes as they left smiling, climbing the staircase to their beds.

Now alone in the room it felt so big and empty, he sat contemplating what to do next "Drink then bed 1 guess" he muttered to himself. Walking into the kitchen he clicked on the kettle and began to stair blankly out of the window. His own reflection bouncing back at him, there was no smile on his face now. He bowed his head, filled his cup with boiling water and began to stir his tea slowly, the spoon clinking loudly on the bright white mug. Walking to his room he hoped someone would still be up, stop him in passing "do you want to watch a film mate?", "were going to play a game you up for it?". But there was know one to be seen on route.

As the bedroom door clicked shut behind him, he closed his door screen and slipped into bed. As though someone had twisted on an old faulty kitchen tap his eyes began to weep tears, streaming down his face one after the other, uncontrollable. The dam that had held so strong and secure all day finally at its breaking point, beginning to let through. Although the room was dark, it was nothing compared with the thoughts and memory's now flooding his head, clouding his mind and judgment with a black smoke.

The mask had now fallen off. This was the real him at the moment, yes, he was able to put on a good show, using the laughter of others as a coping mechanism. If they are happy it makes him happy surely. The truth is by wearing a mask all day, for days and days at a time we grow tired. That mask begins to slip, only by removing that mask permanently can we truly confront what lies beneath. The real him. He can then work hard to get that real him back to a stage where making people laugh is done using a true and unique personality trait and not for self-indulgence. He has been wearing this mask for so long now he has forgotten what the true reflection beneath look like and represents.

As he lay their face pressed hard in to his pillow he thought of a boxer, this was his mind you see. The bell ringing loudly to indicate the next round, face heavily bloody, eyes swollen he staggered to the center of the ring. Punch after punch, jab after jab, uppercut after uppercut a bombardment of pain, hands by his side held by invisible unbreakable chains. Another shot hit hard to the head, Knees shaking he dropped with a thud to the canvas. "get up!", "get up!" he could here himself bellowing in the distance "you're not out yet, get up!"

He awoke suddenly, shaking uncontrollably, thoughts of self-harm and suicide filling his mind. He used the will power he had left to turn over onto his side, reaching out his arm from the comfort and safety of his blanket. Fingers clasped and swept up a photo, his little girl sat having a tea party with Peppa and Georgie Pig, she was his everything, his world, the reason he must keep fighting this constant self-destruct. He kissed it long and hard before balancing it back between two books on his bedside table. Whipping away his tears from his eyes he rolled back over and slowly let them fall shut. Breathing deeply and slowly, each breath getting easier as the seconds past. "I'm not out yet" he whispered allowed to the voices in his head, as he Pulled himself up from the canvas and walked back to the center of the ring.

gloves now raised.

3. A CRIMSON ESCAPE

As he sat on the end of his bed, cold and wet from the shower. His eyes falling on his arm, streaks of blood now seeping from his skin again, like crimson tears. He had inflicted these, his mind finally full, an escape, a release was needed. A bomb inside his head counting down the seconds waiting to implode. He had tried so hard to diffuse, cutting the wires hoping, praying that the clock would stop like in a Hollywood blockbuster. But no matter what wire he cut, what technique he used, the seconds kept on falling down.

Reaching breaking point is a very common phrase, people use it every day in work, family, even with their friends. At some point in life we will all reach this so called breaking point. It is the expression and severity of actions once this point is reach that defines the difference between each individual human being. It may be to express anger at a loved one. To cry in front of your colleagues. Or hit a wall in frustration in front of your friends. These are all expressions that happen so often to us all through life. The majority of the time our feeling will quickly subside, a tranquilizer injected into the body, replacing raw emotion and overwhelming with a serenity of calm. For so many people however, more expression is needed. A shouting match back and forth, a bloody knuckle, an outburst and stream of tears none of these actions will do. In their mind, true physical pain is the only plausible, possible way out. There is something about watching a knife or razor self-generate a thin valley into your own flesh, sending a sensation through your nerves of true pain that shortly diffuses, that gives you refuge from your thoughts. Even for a time in the aftermath you are able to look at them and feel that pain again. It is a stronghold, an army, a defence. The only thing, option that you believe you have... as thoughts of moving that blade to your wrist smash hard in your head, the movement of fingers instead running the knife over and over your skin, slightly deeper with each stroke. Thoughts that you are unable to control, boxed up and put to the back of your mind, slowly evaporating with each sparkle of blood that rises to the surface. These scars however haunt you. You begin to worry about people seeing. We as human beings find it so easy to judge things in which we personally possess no knowledge. Spotting someone you don't even know, you haven't even met with these crimson tattoos lying bare and raw for all to see. We ask why? "Just don't do it?" We as individuals must realise, rationalise and think. It could be something you fixate on, something you yourself would never comprehend doing. So, what does that say about the scarred individual? Are they strange? "Why would you cut yourself?" Here is another view. If you are lucky enough to be able to see visible damage on another and know you have never wanted or felt the need to do that yourself. Show compassion. Self-harm is an expression. Think instead what must be going on in that person's head for their own brain to self-inflict physical pain and anguish on to themselves. Each time you catch a glance and get seen looking, their sleeve will fly down to cover up and conceal. This then stops the worry of people seeing and judging. The other thing you have now started is a train, a thought train bellowing steam as it leaves the station. They are now more aware, thinking of thoughts, times that brought them to point of infliction.

Getting up from his bed he dried off and got changed. As he looked into the mirror he forced a smile "A good day today" he recited to himself aloud. Once breakfast and his morning coffee had been consumed contemplation began, what now? Read a book, tv maybe. Putting his feet up on the sofa his body beginning to relax as he began to watch Jamie Oliver cooking up another mouthwatering dish. His mind now in a good place, no thoughts would bring me down today he told himself. As he continued to watch the meal come together in all its glory, he hummed Fleetwood Mack's you've got to go your own way, his mood upbeat, feet tapping along. The door flew open "Hey, watcha doing?" the voice asked, coming out of his food and musical trance he replied "nothing much, just watching a bit of television" "Have you got any plans today then?" she asked him, he held up his left hand and made a zero with his fingers. "Chill day then?" was the reply "Yep!" he did feel chilled, thoughts locked away safely in his mind, leaving him free to function as normal. He turned back to the celebrity guest now making umming sounds as she ate the perfectly cooked beef. Out of nowhere a question, "how's your arm?" Confused for a second, he wondered what she was referring to. "My arm?" he replied. "Yeah" was her retort. His eyes moving down to rest on the scar torn skin he had thought his sleeves had been concealing. "Fine" he finally answered. "don't do that, just talk to us" was the comeback. As though a power cut had just flicked off all the security his mind had put in place for today, the secure cages and bolted down locks now springing open. Thoughts of sadness, hopelessness and anger rising like a quick tide in his mind. Three words was all it had taken to unleash hours and hours and hours of constraint. He could feel his pulse raising, blood now flowing fast and hard to every vessel in his body. It was like reaching the top of the stairs and closing the stairgate behind you. Only for someone unexpected, hiding in the dark, to sneak out and unlatch it, giving you a gentle push, falling, trying to grab hold of anything without avail.

It took a short while after the conversation for the power to ignite again, every prisoner back in their cage. The day goes on. Roads have speed bumps to keep others safe, life has them so we are able to feel small reminders, jumps, jolts of feelings to make us feel alive.

Please, and I express this in the sincerest of ways, we must think. If you know someone is in a state of distress or can see very visible scars showing how they recently have been. Tread carefully. He managed to turn that spark of energy back on but don't be that spark of energy that turns off somebody's power. As they may not be able to turn it back on.

4 . RELEASE THE KEY

One to one therapy sessions are very tough. Having to go into exact detail about your past, present and future. Dissecting each molecule means raw emotion appears. It rises to the surface hovering behind your eyes, sending your fingers clenching into fists and your breathing speeding like a fast-moving car.

Personally, I find these one to one sessions so rewarding afterwards. Don't get me wrong. You may well leave the room more downbeat, your head drawn and tear stained eyes. What has happened, everything that has brought you here has been exposed, torn open, naked for the professional sitting next to you. What I find however is that you have been able to release these demons, memories, problems. Not onto yourself, but to another. The sandbags on each shoulder start feeling a little lighter with each word.

Group therapy is very different, yet also very similar. You are able to share these same thoughts as the one to one sessions, but your peers are there with you. Sat side by side they are able to become the heavy book-ends to your personal manuscript. They may be sitting in that room with you for completely different reasons, their mind feeling a different type of pain or struggle. Be it drug use, alcohol, anxiety or depression to list just a few. This room, this chair structured circle, becomes a safe haven. Some of the best experiences I have had have been when I have just sat and listened, all preconceptions of drug addicts, alcoholics dissolving like a stock cube under boiling water. You begin to see the person behind these issues, hear what has brought them to this crossroad in life. It is emotion only few will experience during a lifetime, but one I wish more could. Someone who you thought you had no common interest with or shared personality traits all of a sudden says something that strikes like a knife to the heart. "That's me" you tell yourself. Then you repeat it out loud, "that's me, I did that, I went through exactly the same thing". Their face turns to yours, a discussion, meaningful exchange brewing. It is a phrase used a lot, "You are not alone", how true. This person sat next to you, someone you have known a mere two days is in the chair by your side expressing and divulging an experience you are currently going though yourself. After more discussion and reminiscing it becomes clear they got through that problem, issue, time in life. "So, can I, you now say aloud". Tips passed from one brain to another. A gift of experience. Thoughts and past experiences that potentially have the power to armour another's mind, give them a newly found form of mental defence that they never even knew about. The therapist in the room with you is among the best there is, yet this new information could only have passed between two people who have lived through that pain, that difficulty. No textbook can replicate the feeling of depression, the urge for a drink or overwhelming need for that next line of cocaine.

Take everything you can from these sessions, sat in that small circle, face to face with your peers. Speak not only because it will ease the weight off your shoulders but because you could help another deal with their own. It may even be something that allows them over time to relinquish the bags of sand for good. You could well be holding the lost key of someone's happiness. A gift so precious that it may even save a life...

who　　knows　　if　　we　　don't　　share　　it?

5. A DREAM IS NOT YOUR REALITY

"Can I come over and pick my stuff up" she asked him down the phone. Smiling he replied "no problem". Before he knew it, she was grabbing paperwork, photos, shoes and kitchen utensils. He stood there with his daughter holding his leg tightly. "how are you?" was the question he asked. "I'm amazing" she replied. "So much better now that you have left". His heart sank a little as she continued, a lump forming in his throat. "I've been with so many new people, I'm having so much fun, they are so good compared to you. I can't believe I've wasted this much time just sleeping with you!" His hands began to shake, "why are you telling me this?" his voice crackled. "Because you need to know how shit you are." She left the room, he followed, tears now welling in his eyes, small droplets falling onto the wooden floor. "I've had a different one each night" she laughed at him, "you should picture it!" He was transported, arriving in her bedroom tied down being made to watch everything unfold before him. The woman he loved so much screaming with pleasure as the stranger continued, her eyes fixed on him, helplessly sat there. "Keep your eyes open" she shouted. "this is how you fuck someone." He couldn't take it, his emotions getting the better of him. Crying hysterically, every breath nearly impossible to inhale.

He was back in his bed. Blood covered the crisp white sheets, she was stood over him, laughing. "Look at what you have done to yourself" she was pointing to his legs. Every molecule of skin covered in deep cuts. Blood seeping, heart pounding. How could he have self-harmed, he had been asleep. Jumping out of the bed he began to search for evidence, what had he used? All the while she was shouting at him, laughing, "you're so pathetic! I'm off every night getting fucked and you just sit there cutting yourself and picturing it." She let out a long laugh. She was enjoying this. He found a blood-soaked button, it was smashed, sharp edges protruding around its circumference. He had done it. "but how?" he asked her, "because you're scum" she retorted. "you're doing the right thing though! If I were in the same situation, and had to look at your reflection each day, I would deface it."

He was slumped now in the corner of the room a knife in hand, the same knife, "do it then" she bellowed at him, "do it". His hands moved quick as the blade sliced easily through his wrist... lying there his eyes slowly closing, he could just make out the outlines before him... she was there looking at him and smiling, her hand clasped tightly to another, a new man, a man who was holding a smiling little girl, his girl.

Eyes opening suddenly, his room taking focus, each second items of furniture becoming clearer, more in focus. He could feel his heart pumping hard through his pyjama top, bed soaked in sweat and tears. But no blood. Turning to his phone he checked the time. This was real. He was now back in reality, it was a nightmare of the highest order and pain threshold. Breathing heavily, he pulled himself out of the bed and strode purposefully towards his desk. Searching through the piles of paper before finally coming across a pen. Grabbing the first bit of parchment he could find he began to write, words and words pouring out of him, raw unfiltered emotion being transferred from brain and heart to paper. With each letter that appeared before him the pain began to ease. Writing word after word, sentence after sentence, tears splashing the ink beneath him. When he had finally captured each moment of the surreal lifelike experience his brain had just put him through when he was at his most vulnerable, guards down, fast asleep, his breath began to steady. Slowly but surely returning to a normal rate, a rate in which he now controlled.

Writing has been somewhat of a sanctuary to him being able to transfer thoughts of fiction and fact onto a plain piece of crisp white paper with the use of a simple ballpoint pen. This has enabled him to create a space in his mind in which his defences are able to form a counter attack against these punishing, heart wrenching, paralysing thoughts. Writing is the simplest of ways to express our feelings and thoughts. It is something we are taught at such a young age and something we most take for granted. It is almost a guarantee that once you transfer these thoughts to paper your mind will almost immediately begin to re-evaluate and function. It was able to provide him with the tools to realise,

a dream is not your reality.

6. A STRONG CORE

After the tears dry away, everyone's head left with the morning commuter bustle. A time out was needed. It may be to use relaxation, play a game, or a new task completely. After a very hard day of sharing and reliving moments, watching that microfilm over and over in our mind, that brought us here. The next session needed to be light. And light it was.

A challenge set, the gauntlet thrown down. In teams of two, they were tasked with making a bridge of sorts, a bridge that could withstand more weight than that of their opposition. It had to balance between the two large sofas situated in the living area, no central support was allowed. Free standing and strong. Reminding him of what he must be to overcome the difficulties that had taken hold of his every being these past few months.

He and his teammate set to work. Foil, plastic cups, paper and an endless reel for Sellotape their chosen materials. First, they must make it structurally sound. Like the mind our self-belief and foundations, strong and unmoving. Using rolled up scrawls of A1 paper, a frame was soon apparent. Lifting to test was next. Try and test, we don't have to get this right first time. It was found to be less rigid than hoped, a new idea sprung.

Stack and secure plastic cups, one on one, top to bottom, together stronger. Much like the support network that surrounds us so often every day.

After the tedious task of fixing these cups dead centre they began to roll the foil over and over, each sheet adding to the outer protective crust. Now the most important part, they discussed the weights and anchors for each end. This was crucial. The core belief if you like. Without these, the central structure would be redundant. Without our main pillars, holding us up, the backbone of our being, it must be strong. We must be strong. Clay cups filled and rolled into each end of the structure, before lifting the shiny newly erected bridge into place. The anchoring was next. It was clear that the tape used by the opposing team would not be enough. Learn and re-plan he thought. Using the tape, they wound their spiders web of support, round and round the base of the furniture, each time growing stronger still. Once some feeble decoration was applied by his teammate, the challenge began. Tools down, nothing more could be done. First up the weight of a remote control. Both bridges tested, both passing with distinction. Next a book. Again, they stood strong and still. "More" the onlookers called out, two books now, still they maintained strength. However, slight flexes now showing. Once the third was placed a small wobble in the oppositions paper armour. Fear now growing in the eyes of the opponents across the room. It was a board game next! A heavy box. Downfall. Imploding once set, paper buckling like a broken scale as books and boxes shattered to the floor.

So, the win was theirs, now how much would it take. Book after book, game after game, still it stayed strong. The support system proving the deciding factor. How true this is, we as individuals may wobble with the weight of life, expectation after expectation. The books representing work, family, friends, addictions. It was the base of the support that stood strong and unmoving. Believe in yourself, let yourself be shaken from time to time, it won't matter, because you put the work in, you may not have got it right first time, but over time you have become so strong, so empowered that nothing, no matter how heavy or hard, how stressful and tough, can break you. It is your core, your anchor, your foundation for existence and purpose in life.

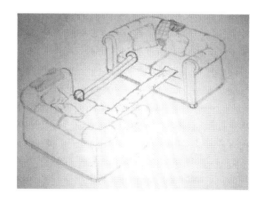

7. WHAT DOES IT MEAN TO BE GRATEFUL?

Sitting there, hand made blade held in his shaking right hand, mind engulfing battle. A constant change of tide, each thought, bad and good on opposing sides of the line, pulling hard, strong in their direction. A moment of pause was needed, both sides exhausted by the constant struggle and fight. This reflection may well be as quick and sudden as thirty seconds, so what advantage, help or performance enhancing insight can our subconscious gather to aid the positive thoughts when the whistle is blown and the battle recommences. The five senses are a great technique and a perfect place to begin. Being grateful for the gift of each one of them. The touch of the cold metal clasped in his hand, the sound of music he had mustered the strength to put on, the taste of his inner cheek as he bit down hard, the sight of scar torn legs, each scar at a different phase of healing, finally the smell of aftershave and cleaning product filling his nostrils. This was the reality he needed to be grateful of. The here and now. What else then? As the timer ticked down slowly, ready to resume the fight. His daughter Molly. He thought of how she had squeezed him last, holding on so as he didn't leave her again. Tears now forming behind his eyes. Then came his family, his dad at his side stood by him hand on his shoulder and aided his recovery back to the present. Then there were his friends, texting and calling him daily, taking time out of their own lives, troubles and situations to see if he was okay.

Beep, beep, beep... as the timer reached the last few seconds. Thoughts good and bad taking up their battle stations, weapons in hand. This gratitude had been realised. He had himself not realised it but there were more thoughts now in the platoon of good. Growing fast and wild like an uncontrollable root or weed, happy memories, laughter, faces of all those close to him, side by side. An alarm sounded and resumption commenced. The battle had begun again, rest now over, hand shaking uncontrollably, sweat and tears dripping off his face onto his scar torn legs. Blade pressed to his skin, held there by an invisible forcefield. Brain directing messages to pull, pull hard and deep, let me feel pain. The heart fighting back, standing ground. These moments, memories, photos of gratitude beginning to overpower the head full of negativity. Wave after wave, water crashed hard and extinguished. Hand now holding steadier with each shake. The door flung open, a woman in front of him now. She reached out and took the blade. Breathing still uncontrollable, he was not sure how he stood and covered the short distance to the chair in his room. Sat listening to her voice. Head still full of the carnage and fight that had just taken place. Her words of thought and caring were so hard to distinguish over a sea of noise, distraction and memories. It didn't matter if his sense now failed him. They had been there when it mattered, alongside the memories and positive feelings. Gratitude without even knowing, had secretly come to his aid, had been his cavalry. It had helped him win this battle. He must now stay resilient. He must use it again and again, over and over. Could it be possible that it may well gift him the necessary tools he has been searching so tediously for? May this gift, this amazing realisation win him the war and restrain his negative crusaders for good?

8. YOU GET OUT WHAT YOU PUT IN

He has already done the hardest task of all. He has reached out, to a family member, friend and professional. He, no one else has made those first initial steps to aid his recovery. This in itself means that no matter what state his mind is currently in, the place he now resides is the best place for him.

Day to day at the Priory can be really tough, He would often sit on the end of his bed for more than twenty minutes at a time just to conger up the energy and confidence to leave his room, walk to the kitchen, quickly grab a glass of water and hurry back. Each day at a time, he was told when he first arrived and how true this is. It may not feel like it, no sudden change of wind or season taking hold and re-directing his thoughts and actions. However slowly over time his confidence grew. There is no set formula for how long your recovery will take, yes you may be on a twenty-eight program for addiction, or the insurance may be playing it by ear, one or two weeks at a time. He was very fortunate, upon his first few days here he got talking to another patient, someone who was now closing in on his leaving date, as the conversation progressed it came to fruition that he had been in a very simpler place, he two attempting to take his own life. As he sat there and listened to every word his mind wondering, thinking, "he seems fine, happy even". The truth was he had gotten out of this whole experience what he put in, he spoke in depth and detail about how hard he worked, every piece of homework, every form or diary sheet filled in even practicing mindfulness exercises at any available free time he had.

There is a very common misconception about a rehab/recovery centre. Lots of people may look at it selfishly from the outside "he's off having a jolly, no work no stress" how wrong these small-minded people are. He was being put through his paces every day, session after session digging deeper and deeper with each sentence shared. Being made to relive and picture the worst moments of his life. Brain in constant fight mode, undecided as to what mood to put you in, how to define your day. The first thing he found the hardest was actually just getting up and getting himself to the morning group. You will learn that all therapy groups are in fact optional, you do not have to attend if you wish not to. But trust me when I say this, you must. His feelings of doubt and isolation were so strong, "just let time do its work" he would often think alone in his room. Your room at the Priory is a very strange thing. It is your own private space, a space that allows you to be free from the cameras, from people. After time though your brain quickly cottons on. Like an assassin who researches the best possible time to execute the kill. "when are they most vulnerable" and that is when you are alone in your room. Very quickly you become more isolated by the hour your brain relishing and feeding off thoughts of self-pity and doubt. It is imperative you fight back and work hard. During these times he would work constantly when in his room, taking on the advice from someone who had already been thorough this and was now coming out of the other side. Word after word, expression after expression he would jot down, feelings, thoughts, all new weapons he had now been given to use. He downloaded an app called Headspace. An app in which you can take that time out and listen to as you practice mindfulness. Don't get it wrong, he was a dubious and sceptical about this practice more than anyone, all that meditation and humming sounds, load of rubbish. How wrong he was, it taught him the ability to bring himself back to the here and now, back from memory's or thoughts of despair. This was vital in his recovery.

Communal areas are here for a reason, try your best and it is hard and defiantly easier said than done but if you want to do some work, or watch a little television do this away from your room, don't give your brain that opportunity to exploit that isolation and use the vulnerability that comes with it. Most of all practice. Practice everything you get thought, over and over, you really can't do too much. Think of it as training your mind. If you were to run a marathon you would be out daily putting in the hours on the road, trainers getting lighter and easier to lift with each day that passes so that when that day comes, and your stood on that start line ready to leave the safety of the priory you can say to yourself "this is it, I'm ready" because you put the work in. If a household appliance was to break you would not simply keep clicking it on daily hoping it will miraculously fix itself and resume working. It needs to be fixed, you, he, all your peers need to be fixed. You and only you have the capability to do that. To find that inner strength, side by side with people next to you, your pace setters if you like. Preparing yourself for that race day, you need to be ready for it.

Try, and it really is so hard but try your upmost to embrace every class, everyone to one, every bit of alone time. Getting up in the morning, getting changed, having a coffee or breakfast, walking into that room full of people you don't really know is so difficult. But that's the hard part done, you are now there, sat, pen in hand work sheet after work sheet set in front of you ready for you to absorb. Share, share everything, sitting on that chair just listening won't be enough in the long run, muster up that small bit of inner believe, that minuscule bit of courage and determination you have left and use it to take part properly and fully, to engage and learn. It cannot be stressed enough That you get out what you put in. Make sure you don't leave that room at the end of a class regretting you didn't speak up or say more. Everyone around you is in the same boat, each slightly different but each road has lead you all to be sat side by side in that room together. Let the therapy team do what they are so very brilliant at, helping you. They like every other profession need tools to work with, there tool is your mind, so open it and let them set to work giving you every chance to come out of this experience a different person. You have tried to fix this yourself but to no avail, you now have the help, guidance and support needed you just have to use it. Use it as much as you can because no matter how difficult it is, by doing so you are able to re-find yourself and re-determine the outcome and future of your life.

9. YOU CAN'T GIVE UP

He was now entering his fifth week. The weekend has been a bad one, Sunday night his thoughts had been let loose, spiraling his mind out of control, making him to succumb to the urges he had been fighting off for so long now. Self-Harming. Over the course of the day he had calmly gone into his bathroom and accumulated forty-eight cuts over his legs and arms. Tens of blood stained toilet paper sheets lay at his feet. Blood still seeping from some of the deeper cuts. As he sat there on the bathroom floor he looked at his skin, his own skin that he had ripped apart cut after cut, each one deliberately deeper, more painful. He didn't care anymore, the techniques he had learnt over the past five weeks had prolonged this moment, had stopped in self-harming over seventy percent of the time. But this thirty percent still remained. As he began to cry, feelings of frustration, anger and hopelessness filling his mind. "fix me!" he shouted allowed to the walls in his bathroom. "I can't do this anymore" he was exhausted. He had put in hours after hours of work, his mind fighting battle after battle yet these memories still got through, they had broken the front line down piece by piece. Everyone would tell him to think about himself, what is my life, who is James Richard Allen. But he didn't know, he had been searching so long and hard to find these answers but to no avail. He can't go on anymore. Looking down at his wrists he removed his watch from his left hand and held the blade over it...shaking uncontrollably now tears falling on his skin one after the other a constant flow. Gasping for breath he shouted again "I can't do it" he wanted someone to help him, he knew someone would cheek on him soon, they did so every fifteen minutes. Just hold out he said, someone will come. It was like someone had paused time, he was alone, his enemy shinny and silver clutched in his right hand. "no" he let out. "no, no, no" he managed to say in between breathes of air. His right fingers began to loosen, hand tilting the blade dropped to the floor. He would go home tomorrow he thought. He would just get out of this bubble and get on with his life, if after a few days it did not subside, he could end it then.

Later that night he got into bed, calm and collected. Mind made. Getting up the next morning was easy, he had no doubt he wanted to leave, he would go to morning group and speak with his therapist afterwards to inform him of his decision. Sitting there he wrote about his day yesterday, no lies, pure honesty. He spoke allowed to everyone how he was feeling, he wasn't getting better he was just prolonging, he didn't have the answers and no one else seemed to have them either. "could we have a one to one today?" asked his lead therapist. Why not he thought, may as well. In the hour that followed he sat around in a trance. Not sad, not upset, not angry. Just an empty shipping vessel lost at sea without a crew.

He sat in the room waiting for the therapist to arrive, thoughts continuing to confirm this was the right thing, legs still throbbing, arms beginning to scab over. The therapist sat down opposite him and gave him a look meaningful heartfelt look" this relaxed him a little, someone did care, he could see that. But he knew that already, everyone cared, his family, friends, everyone, but couldn't they see it didn't matter. The talking began, going back over the same things that had brought him here, although something was strangely different, more detail was appearing, his memory bank seeming to be distributing much clearer precise images. As he kept talking right up to the present he started feeling strange. A really odd feeling. Then the therapist said something about his daughter, he's not sure exactually what it was but it was something. It is by far the most amazing, scary and enlightening feeling he had ever felt. As though suddenly someone had opened the dust filled curtains and let the warm soft summer light flood his mind. He could see things now that were not there before. Gaps now filled with laughter and happiness. It was as though the old life script he had been so determined to hold on to, clasping it so tightly had finally ripped away. In its place a new bright white sheet of paper. He had the pen. He could start again this would be his script, no one else's, he wouldn't share this with anybody. But he would write more scripts, lots of them, piles of them. A script for him and his daughter, him and his family, his friends, his job...they would be stacked high to the ceiling, why live life off one script your entire life when you can write so many. It didn't matter now if one by one they got ripped up, cast aside. No one could touch his script. Him. This would be a foundation like he had never had before. A foundation that was completely impenetrable.

How close he had come to giving up, maybe it was reaching rock bottom that made him look upwards. I don't know. But he had worked for this, hours and hours of work over and over, repetition over repetition. That is why he had said yes to the one to one. That is why and how he had found himself. So why can't you? It will be so hard. It will feel impossible at times, truly impossible, but don't give up! Keep fighting, the real you is in there somewhere, go find it, let people help you find it, because when you do for the first time in your life you may well feel the most amazing feeling. A feeling that has more capability than any textbook exercise or words of advice, a feeling so strong you may even be able to put these demons on a tight leash, lock them away, still there but now under complete control, your control. Please I implore you, don't give up. You can't give up.

10. LIGHTBULB MOMENT

He found himself once again at rock bottom. A place that had become so familiar to him in the last six weeks. A place full of darkness and despair, bitterness and isolation. He had visited this space so many times now, stood staring at the rope that had been gifted down to him through tear-stricken eyes, his energy levels now fading in each passing second. Is it worth the climb? So far was the tedious pull to happiness and peace.

He had tried, over and over but to no avail. Sometimes he would reach resting points, glimmers of hope, an opportunity to regather, refocus. However again and again he would fall short. The rope being pulled away from him know matter how hard he squeezed. Falling with a thud, scars appearing each time, deeper and more permanent than before. Would he ever reach the top? A question before now he had been certain he knew the answer to, yes. Yet after so many recurring falls, so many failed attempts was it really worth another go? Putting himself through the pain and mental strength required.

He sat there in the darkness. The cold damp floor seeping into his dusty clothes. Fixated, eyes unmoving on the end of the rope before him, as if it may vanish if he even dared to bink. Crying, shaking, heart beat racing he unbelievably found the energy to pick himself up off the floor. Bloody and scar ridden he stumbled over to the rope. His brain now barking internal instructions, orders at his hands and arms to reach out and grab it. Yet still they remained motionless at his side, unmoving and unresponsive. He attempted again and again yet he found himself routed and paralysed. Anger and frustration now rising, the feeling of despair pleaded with his mind to sit back down and give in for good. "No!" his voice suddenly amplified, echoing of every wall all the way to the top. "Grab it!" his brain bellowed, "grab it!" ... suddenly his arms flew upward, hands now clasped tightly around the thousand of small pieces of material. "there stronger as one" he whispered in the darkness. Slowly he began to climb again, feet occasionally slipping on the wall, hands beginning to burn with pain and exhaustion. After what seemed like an eternity he came to a clearing in the stone.

Letting go of the rope he climbed inside. Breathing uncontrollable, face covered in glistening moisture. Looking down at his hands, blood now seeping from them. I can't go on he thought, yet another failed attempt, yet another drop into the darkness was surely the only plausible outcome. Breathing deeply, he noticed the air was cleaner now, each breath filling his lungs with the energy he needed. It was brighter to, he could make out the stony, wet, mould ridden complexion of the wall. "there is hope" a voice whispered to him. Startled he spun around...emptiness, he was alone. The voice had come from within, his inner strength.

Hands now pulling the rope tight, feet set, he began to climb again. Bright light now visible, never before had he come so far, he could hear voices, he was sure there were real, positive in fact. With a new found inner strength he pulled harder. Up and up he climbed his eyes wandering, chest constantly trying to keep going, lactic acid now flowed to every muscle, every cell in his body experiencing excruciating pain. His hands began to loosen, legs slipping, desperate to find a foot hold, he began to fall, rope between his hands, unable to grab a hold. "come on" he screamed and his hands suddenly found purchase. Feet back in the hold. His head fell downwards, he had fallen so far yet again. He did not have the energy to carry on. The will power fading from each molecule of sweet seeping from his skin. "just drop" came the darkness "let it go", "you can't do it", "you tried". He was out.

The inner strength he had found before seemed to be screaming, lost in the distance now. It was still there though, that had to mean something. Looking up reality began to sink in, like a stone thrown in water "it's too far" he gasped. Looking at his hands now, his grip loosening with each blink of his eyes. Suddenly a jolt, he clung on, another jolt followed. He was traveling upwards now, but how? Holding onto the rope was imperative. Life...or...death. his fingers clamped harder and harder, all pain and suffering being blown away by this new-found hope. There was a breeze now, he was soring upwards, rope and body covering meter by meter every second. Could he do it...ten meters or so, all that was left. Bright light now blinding his rectors. Squinting hard, he was so close. And suddenly it stopped. Still, swaying "no, no, no" he pleaded, "no not now!" "not now please!"

A thought flicked into his mind, his lightbulb moment. "It must be me he whispered. His help, his saviours had got him so far, but he knew now only he could get himself free, free from this place, this darkness. He reached up his right arm, stretching desperately for the ledge. His fingers found grass, holding on with everything, he pulled his left-hand round. The touch and smell of grass now taking a hold. He pulled, elbows bending and bleeding. His face falling flat onto the lawn. A defining raw, filled the air. People surrounding him, all holding the rope. There was his dad, his mum, his sister. Friends, therapists and peers. They had pulled him, they had helped save him. Everyone together.

Falling to his knees, eyes welling with tears. He smiled and began to laugh, they all laughed with him. Embracing him with open arms. This was one of the happiest moments of his life. He would never forget that place, it will always be with him, it may even pop up some days, but he controls it now, he knows the way out.

The crowd of people separated, a small girl running at him, hair bouncing, smile beaming, "welcome home daddy" she shouted. As they embraced, kissing her forehead and squeezing her tight, he whispered "Daddy's home for good now my baby girl!"

ABOUT THE AUTHOR

My Name Is James Allen. In February 2018 I attempted to take my own life. This is a part of my story. I hope it may be able to help you in some way.

Printed in Great Britain
by Amazon

50187342R00031